KINGFISHER KNOWLE E

SPEED MACHINES

AND OTHER RECORD-BREAKING VEHICLES

Miranda Smith

Foreword by

James Dyson

KINGFISHER

KINGFISHER

First published 2009 by Kingfisher
This edition first published 2011 by Kingfisher
an imprint of Macmillan Children's Books
a division of Macmillan Publishers Limited
20 New Wharf Road, London N1 9RR
Basingstoke and Oxford
www.panmacmillan.com

Associated companies throughout the world

ISBN 978-0-7534-1986-1

9 8 7 6 5 4 3 2 1
1TR/1010/WKT/UG/140MA

A CIP catalogue record for this book is available from the British Library.

Printed in China

Contents

NOTE TO READERS

The website addresses listed in this book are correct at the time of going to print. However, due to the ever-changing nature of the internet, website addresses and content can change. Websites can contain links that are unsuitable for children. The publisher cannot be held responsible for changes in website addresses or content, or for information obtained through third-party websites. We strongly advise that internet searches should be supervised by an adult.

GO FURTHER...

INFORMATION PANEL KEY:

websites and further reading

career paths

places to visit

▼ In northern Canada, a truck approaches the frozen surface of a lake along the route of the longest ice road in the world.

Foreword

On 7 February 2005, I became the fastest person to sail round the world alone. Incredibly, I had broken what many (including me) thought was an unbreakable record, racing round the planet in my 23-metre trimaran *B&Q* in 71 days, 14 hours, 18 minutes and 33 seconds.

It all began at the age of four, when I was introduced to sailing by my Aunt Thea. Stepping onboard her boat *Cabaret* for the first time triggered something inside me that has never left. It was the start of a passion for sailing and the water that has lasted my whole life!

As a kid I dreamed of sailing solo around the world, and I spent a huge amount of time reading about famous sailors such as Sir Francis Chichester (1901–72) and Sir Robin Knox-Johnston (born 1939). I was so inspired by them that I even saved up my lunch money to buy my first boat! I loved the freedom that sailing gave me out on the water, with the prospect of being able to sail to wherever I wanted in the world.

I am absolutely fascinated by learning, and I always want to push myself to learn more about sailing and to really understand the boats I am sailing on. I am also quite competitive and want to race my boats as fast as possible, so trying to break records was a natural progression for me.

Records are set to be broken, however, and in January 2008, Frenchman Francis Joyon took back his solo non-stop round-the-world record. I really had to give everything to beat his 2004 record, but now he has bettered mine by 14 days through a combination of a bigger, faster boat, ideal weather and outstanding seamanship.

Francis's journey was also a way for him to send a message regarding the planet and its preservation. He relied only on clean energies such as wind and solar power and did not have an engine aboard his trimaran, which brilliantly shows what can be done. High-speed travel has enabled us to see that the world is not really all that big after all, and that we have an urgent need to protect it – apart from anything, so that future generations can set their own speed records!

I hope that all the amazing stories about record-breaking in this book will inspire you too, so that one day you can break your own record. If, like Francis Joyon, you can do it using clean energies, then that would be truly awesome!

Go for it!

Ellen MacArthur, British yachtswoman who in 2005 broke the record for the fastest solo non-stop voyage around the world, on her first attempt.

CHAPTER 1

Land transport

The air is full of dust, the ground vibrates and there is a deafening scream as engines shoot past along the racetrack. There is nothing as exciting as superfast Formula One cars battling to win a race on a hot summer's day!

Since the earliest times, people have competed to reach the finishing line first. The invention of new forms of transport and the development of new technologies in the 19th and 20th centuries meant that people and machines could work together to achieve feats and speeds that had been impossible before. Every year, history is made and new records are broken. Only the best reach their goal, whether as a cyclist in the gruelling Tour de France, a trucker on the dusty Dakar Rally trail, or a motorcyclist battling for a podium place in the MotoGP World Championship.

British Formula One star Lewis Hamilton leads the field in his McLaren MP4/23 at the 2008 German Grand Prix.

▲ Former test astronaut Gary Gabelich drives the *Blue Flame* to 1,001.47km/h on Bonneville Salt Flats, USA. The rocket-powered, bullet-shaped car broke the land speed record on 23 October 1970. The *Blue Flame* was 11.3m long. It was fuelled with a highly explosive mixture of liquid natural gas and hydrogen peroxide, so it literally rode on a blue jet of flame.

High-speed travel

On 15 October 1997, RAF fighter pilot Andy Green drove *Thrust SSC* (SuperSonic Car) into the record books at an extraordinary 1,227.99km/h. He made two runs in the Black Rock Desert, Nevada, USA, breaking the sound barrier both times. This amazing vehicle has two Phantom jet engines that take about 30 seconds to get *Thrust* up to supersonic speeds. *Thrust SSC* was designed by the previous record-holder, Richard Noble, who had reached 1,019.47km/h in *Thrust 2*.

Obsessed with speed

People are always pushing boundaries, and the men who have broken the world land speed record have pushed them further than most. During the 1960s, the world land speed record passed backwards and forwards as two Americans fought it out on Bonneville Salt Flats. Art Arfons took the title three times in *Green Monster*, while Craig Breedlove triumphed five times in *Spirit of America*. Their dominance was broken when, in 1970, Gary Gabelich zoomed to victory in the *Blue Flame*.

▶ *Thrust SSC* was the result of two and a half years of research followed by around 100,000 hours of construction. It is the first car to use two turbojets and weighs 10 tonnes. It can accelerate from standstill to 160km/h in four seconds. And, by using very strong ribbon parachutes, *Thrust SSC* is slowed to a speed at which the brakes can be used safely.

aerodynamic shape like a twin-jet fighter aircraft with the wings removed

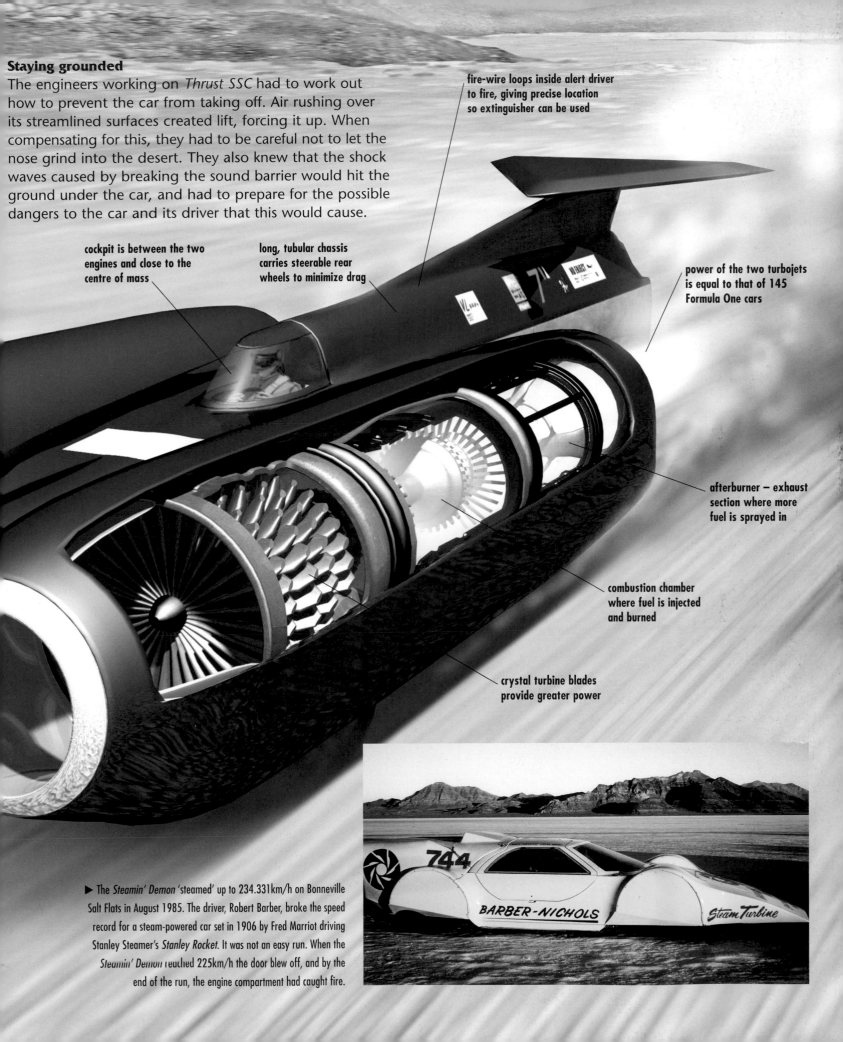

Staying grounded

The engineers working on *Thrust SSC* had to work out how to prevent the car from taking off. Air rushing over its streamlined surfaces created lift, forcing it up. When compensating for this, they had to be careful not to let the nose grind into the desert. They also knew that the shock waves caused by breaking the sound barrier would hit the ground under the car, and had to prepare for the possible dangers to the car and its driver that this would cause.

fire-wire loops inside alert driver to fire, giving precise location so extinguisher can be used

cockpit is between the two engines and close to the centre of mass

long, tubular chassis carries steerable rear wheels to minimize drag

power of the two turbojets is equal to that of 145 Formula One cars

afterburner – exhaust section where more fuel is sprayed in

combustion chamber where fuel is injected and burned

crystal turbine blades provide greater power

▶ The *Steamin' Demon* 'steamed' up to 234.331km/h on Bonneville Salt Flats in August 1985. The driver, Robert Barber, broke the speed record for a steam-powered car set in 1906 by Fred Marriot driving Stanley Steamer's *Stanley Rocket*. It was not an easy run. When the *Steamin' Demon* reached 225km/h the door blew off, and by the end of the run, the engine compartment had caught fire.

The 'fastest man on Earth'

On 10 December 1954, Captain John Stapp of the US Air Force became the fastest man in the world – a record that has still not been broken. Scientist Stapp used himself as a guinea-pig to test the effects of acceleration and deceleration (g-force) on the human body. In *Sonic Wind No.1*, a rocket-propelled sled built out of welded tubes, he reached a speed of 1,017km/h.

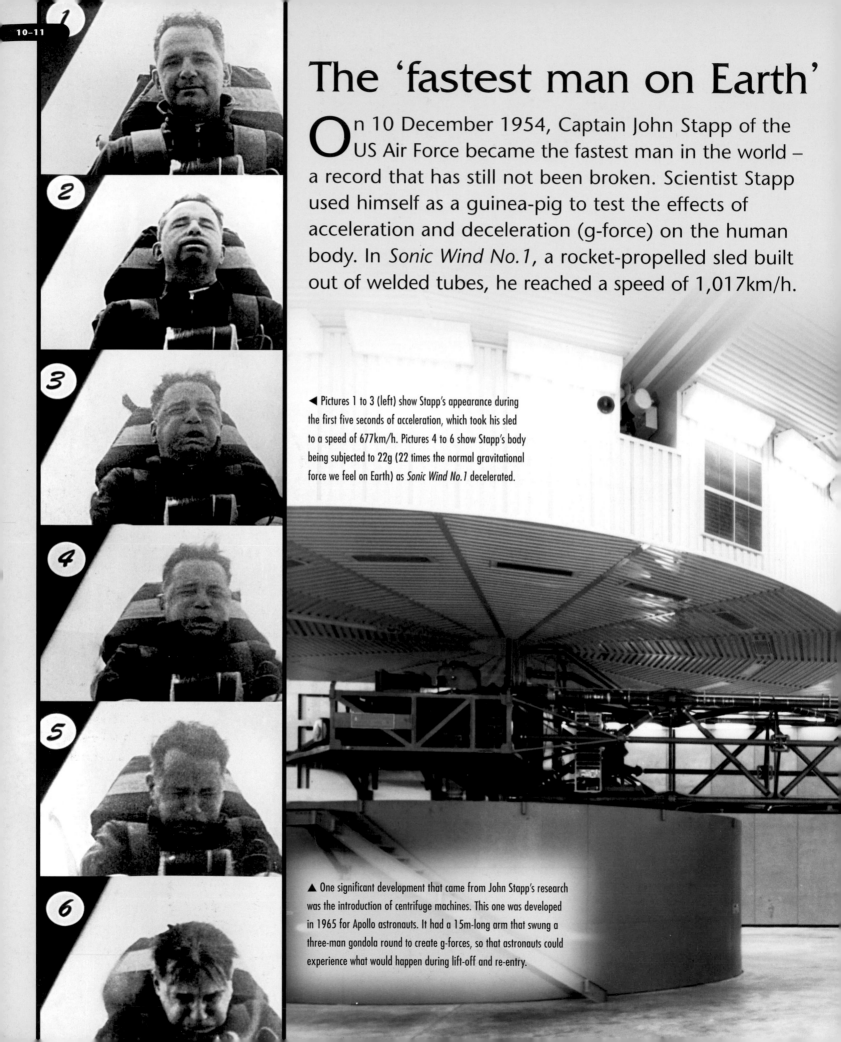

◀ Pictures 1 to 3 (left) show Stapp's appearance during the first five seconds of acceleration, which took his sled to a speed of 677km/h. Pictures 4 to 6 show Stapp's body being subjected to 22g (22 times the normal gravitational force we feel on Earth) as *Sonic Wind No.1* decelerated.

▲ One significant development that came from John Stapp's research was the introduction of centrifuge machines. This one was developed in 1965 for Apollo astronauts. It had a 15m-long arm that swung a three-man gondola round to create g-forces, so that astronauts could experience what would happen during lift-off and re-entry.

Aviation breakthrough

John Stapp was a qualified doctor who was determined to find ways to protect pilots at very high altitudes. In his research, he had already discovered how to stop pilots getting 'the bends' – deadly bubbles that form in the bloodstream at great heights and depths. By experimenting on himself, he found that if the pilots breathed pure oxygen for 30 minutes before take-off, they would not suffer from the bends at all.

▶ The record for the fastest speed travelled on the Moon was set on 23 April 1972. US astronaut John Young drove *Apollo 16*'s Lunar Rover at a speed of 16.99km/h in what came to be known as the 'Grand Prix run'.

Dangerous testing

In 1947, Stapp was flight surgeon to US test pilot Chuck Yeager when Yeager broke the sound barrier in a Bell X-1 aircraft at Mach 1. Afterwards, Stapp planned his rocket-sled experiments to develop a harness that would hold pilots safely in g-force conditions. The first sled was called *Gee Whiz*. During the tests, Stapp lost fillings, fractured ribs, broke his wrist twice and damaged his eyes.

▼ *Sonic Wind No.1*, Stapp's second rocket-powered sled, is seen here in action on its record-making run at Holloman Air Force Base in New Mexico in 1954. It ran along a 610m-long track. At one end were sets of hydraulic brakes that slowed the sled from 240 to 120km/h in just one-fifth of a second.

sensors on harness measured g-force when rocket came to a sudden stop

A winning formula

Motor racing is one of the most exciting of all sports, and the annual Formula One world championship inspires millions of fans all over the world. The cars are the most advanced technologically – and the most expensive. The race is for open-wheelers – cars that are specially built and have their wheels outside the body of the car. The drivers compete to become the World Drivers' Champion, while their crack team of engineers aims to win the World Constructors' trophy.

▲ In contrast to Formula One cars, early stock cars were ordinary cars off the production line with engines that had been finely tuned. Today, the cars competing in the very popular NASCAR races in the USA (above) have eight-cylinder engines and travel round an oval track at over 300km/h.

diffuser sucks air out of the back at high speed

like front wing and underbody, rear wing generates downforce, improving grip on road

barge boards push air towards back of car

some air travels through, cooling engine

air is channelled around front wing

▲ Everything about the design of Formula One racing cars is aimed at helping the car to move smoothly. The more streamlined a car is – the better the airflow around and through the car – the faster it will go. Some Formula One cars can travel at speeds of more than 350km/h.

Racing start
Formula One racing usually takes place on purpose-built racetracks, and two cars from each team take part. There is a qualifying round to decide the line-up on the grid, and who holds pole position – the best place from which to start the race. The cars are made from carbon fibre, which is lightweight but strong. They can accelerate from 0 to 100km/h in under three seconds.

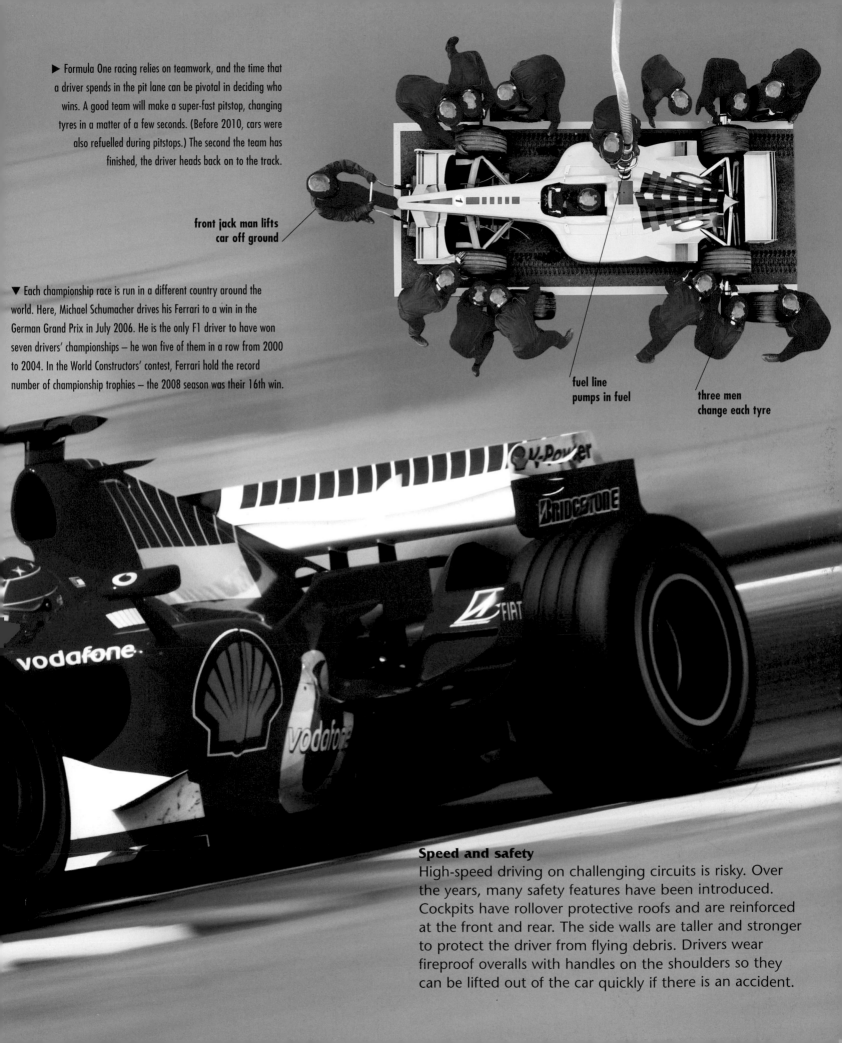

▶ Formula One racing relies on teamwork, and the time that a driver spends in the pit lane can be pivotal in deciding who wins. A good team will make a super-fast pitstop, changing tyres in a matter of a few seconds. (Before 2010, cars were also refuelled during pitstops.) The second the team has finished, the driver heads back on to the track.

front jack man lifts car off ground

▼ Each championship race is run in a different country around the world. Here, Michael Schumacher drives his Ferrari to a win in the German Grand Prix in July 2006. He is the only F1 driver to have won seven drivers' championships – he won five of them in a row from 2000 to 2004. In the World Constructors' contest, Ferrari hold the record number of championship trophies – the 2008 season was their 16th win.

fuel line pumps in fuel

three men change each tyre

Speed and safety

High-speed driving on challenging circuits is risky. Over the years, many safety features have been introduced. Cockpits have rollover protective roofs and are reinforced at the front and rear. The side walls are taller and stronger to protect the driver from flying debris. Drivers wear fireproof overalls with handles on the shoulders so they can be lifted out of the car quickly if there is an accident.

Rallying

In June 1907, five cars set off from Peking (now Beijing) to travel to Paris, a distance of 17,700km. The race took them 61 days. Then in January 1911, the first Monte Carlo Rally took place. Just 23 cars started from six cities around Europe, and only 16 made it to Monte Carlo. These two events marked the birth of international rallying, now a popular motorsport on many continents.

▶ Rallies are long-distance races that take place on public or private roads, over several days or weeks, and often through different countries. The driver and co-driver travel in a series of stages over very rough terrain. The vehicles are usually specially adapted, like this Subaru Impreza WRC, which is being driven through Portugal by Petter Solberg of Norway in round six of the World Rally Championship in 2007.

▲ Every February, one of only two rallies held on snow takes place in Sweden. Originally called the 'Rally to the Midnight Sun', it became part of the World Rally Championship in 1973. This rally is usually won by Swedes and Finns, but in 2004, Frenchman Sébastien Loeb, with co-driver Daniel Elena from Monaco, drove a Citroën Xsara to victory (above).

▶ Terrifying sandstorms, high dunes, rocks and mud are among the many obstacles that face the competitors in the gruelling Dakar Rally. Here, France's Cyril Despres rides his KTM to victory on the seventh stage of the 2007 Dakar Rally between Zouerat and Atar in the western Sahara Desert.

The Dakar Rally

The first Dakar Rally ran from Paris, France, down through Spain to Dakar in Senegal on the west coast of Africa. The route varies from year to year, but covers up to 15,000km and usually ends in Dakar. It is an off-road endurance race with classes for bikes, cars and trucks. The vehicles have to cross some very difficult mountainous and desert terrain.

The World Rally Championship

From 1973, this series of rallies has been run by the *Fédération Internationale de l'Automobile* (FIA), the international governing body for many motor-racing events. Every year, the series includes up to 16 rallies around the world. At the end there is a winning driver and a champion manufacturer. In 2009, Sébastien Loeb of France won his sixth world championship in a row. In the same year, the manufacturer's prize went to Citroën for the second year running.

In the estuary of the River Yangtze near Shanghai, China, the world's largest tunnelling machine – the Double Shield TBM – pushed two three-lane motorway tubes through clay, silt and sand at a rate of 400m a month. The Hushan Expressway opened in 2009.

Mountain movers

Some truly extraordinary working machines have been specially built to help with heavy tasks. Giant tunnel borers create road and rail tunnels that travel under seas and through mountains. Ultra-class dumper trucks ferry loads of up to 345 tonnes at a time. Giant excavators help to move actual mountains of earth and rocks in open-air mines.

▼ The Bagger 288 is used to clear earth and rocks from open-air sites in Germany so that coal can be mined. Its blade (inset) has 18 buckets that rotate, picking up earth and rocks at a rate of 10m per minute before tipping this 'overburden' onto a long conveyor belt that carries it away.

21.6m-wide bucket wheel excavates 2,500 truckloads a day

overburden travels along conveyor belts

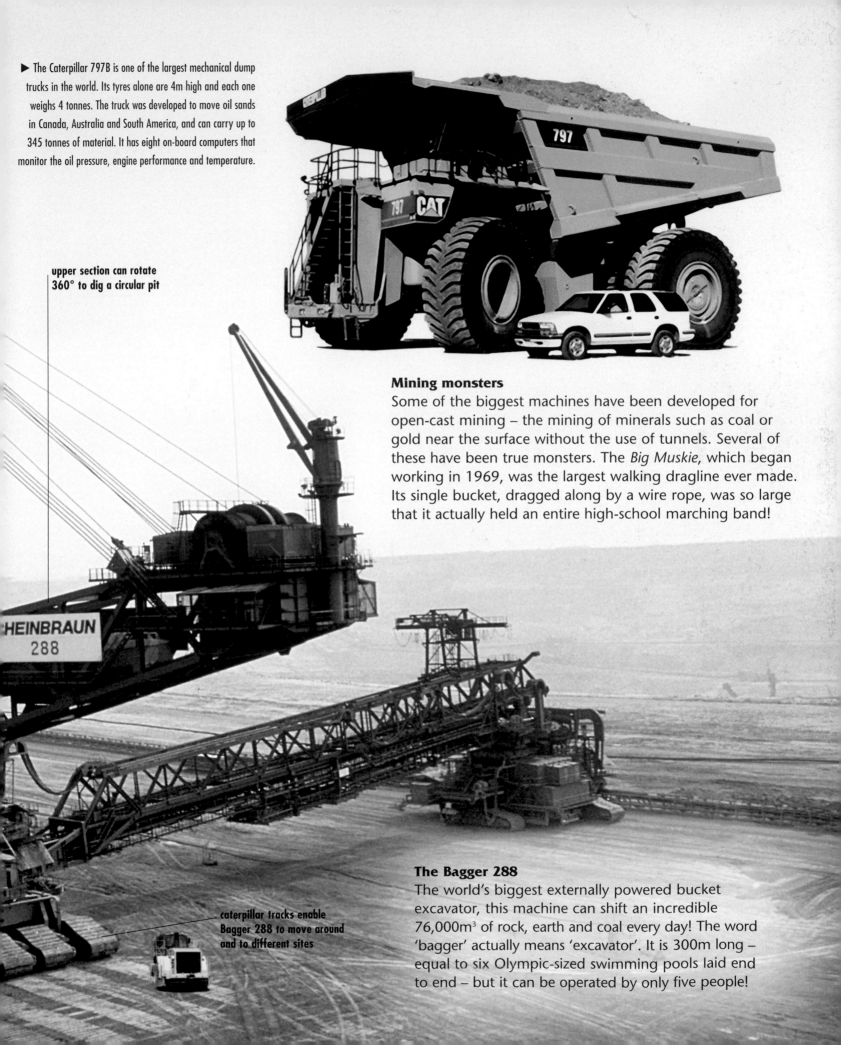

▶ The Caterpillar 797B is one of the largest mechanical dump trucks in the world. Its tyres alone are 4m high and each one weighs 4 tonnes. The truck was developed to move oil sands in Canada, Australia and South America, and can carry up to 345 tonnes of material. It has eight on-board computers that monitor the oil pressure, engine performance and temperature.

upper section can rotate 360° to dig a circular pit

HEINBRAUN
288

Mining monsters

Some of the biggest machines have been developed for open-cast mining – the mining of minerals such as coal or gold near the surface without the use of tunnels. Several of these have been true monsters. The *Big Muskie*, which began working in 1969, was the largest walking dragline ever made. Its single bucket, dragged along by a wire rope, was so large that it actually held an entire high-school marching band!

caterpillar tracks enable Bagger 288 to move around and to different sites

The Bagger 288

The world's biggest externally powered bucket excavator, this machine can shift an incredible 76,000m³ of rock, earth and coal every day! The word 'bagger' actually means 'excavator'. It is 300m long – equal to six Olympic-sized swimming pools laid end to end – but it can be operated by only five people!

Wheeled monsters

There are some truly monstrous trucks out there. A monster truck is a vehicle that has been built or modified so that it has very large wheels and suspension – the part that links the body to the wheels. These sports vehicles take part in competitions and displays that often include jumping over large obstacles. The very first monster truck of all was *Bigfoot*, driven by American Bob Chandler in the 1970s.

▼ The Bigfoot series of monster trucks have set extraordinary records. In 1999, *Bigfoot 14* became the fastest monster truck, reaching a speed of 111.5km/h. At the same event, it set a world record for long jump by hurtling 61.57m over a 727 jet!

Safe monsters

There are many built-in safety features in the modern versions of monster trucks. Most have three kill switches – one of which is remotely controlled by an official race observer. The switches turn off the engine and electrics if there is an accident or rollover. Drivers sit in the centre of the cab and are protected by a rollcage. They wear eye protection, neck collars, helmets and fire-retardant suits.

► Until monster trucks came on the scene, travelling over obstacles and crushing them was something that was normally done only by the caterpillar tracks of tanks in war zones. This anti-aircraft missile system's caterpillar tracks can carry it over all kinds of terrain. The TOR-M1 is a Transporter Launcher Vehicle (TLV) that is able to launch surface-to-air guided missiles.

Monster wheels

Monster trucks have lightweight bodies made of fibreglass over a tubular steel frame, supported by very large wheels. The wheels are the kind made for heavy machinery such as fertilizer spreaders or other farm machinery. The trucks drive right over all kinds of obstacles, especially rows of smaller cars, so the tyres have to be extremely tough. They travel up and over the obstacles, crushing them as they go.

▲ To make sure that other monster trucks could not lay claim to be the largest, Bob Chandler put 3m-tall tyres on *Bigfoot 4*. Then, in 1986, he built *Bigfoot 5* specially to take these tyres. Finally, in 2002, *Bigfoot 5* (above) was officially given the title of the 'World's Tallest, Widest and Heaviest Monster Truck'.

Ice road trucking

Ice road trucking is one of the world's most dangerous jobs. When the lakes of northern Canada freeze over in winter, truckers have only two to three months to get a year's supply of equipment and food to the diamond mines northeast of the town of Yellowknife in the Northwest Territories. Their heavy 18-wheeler rigs carry vast loads in freezing temperatures along purpose-built frozen highways. If for any reason their engines stop or the ice cracks, the truckers will almost certainly die.

▲ Before any rigs can run, a 560-km ice highway has to be created across permafrost and frozen lakes. The Hägglund BV206 (above) is an incredible amphibious vehicle that is able to travel on any terrain. It exerts only half the ground pressure of a single human footprint, and is used to mark out a safe route on the thickest ice. It can even pull itself out if the ice cracks!

▶ An even surface on the ice roads is of vital importance for the truckers that travel along them. The ice cracks and groans all the time beneath the wheels of the heavy vehicles. To begin with, a team of snowploughs sculpt the ice roads, scraping the snow to the side as they move along. Over the following months, they continue to maintain the roads, even drilling holes in the ice to flood it so that it refreezes and becomes thicker.

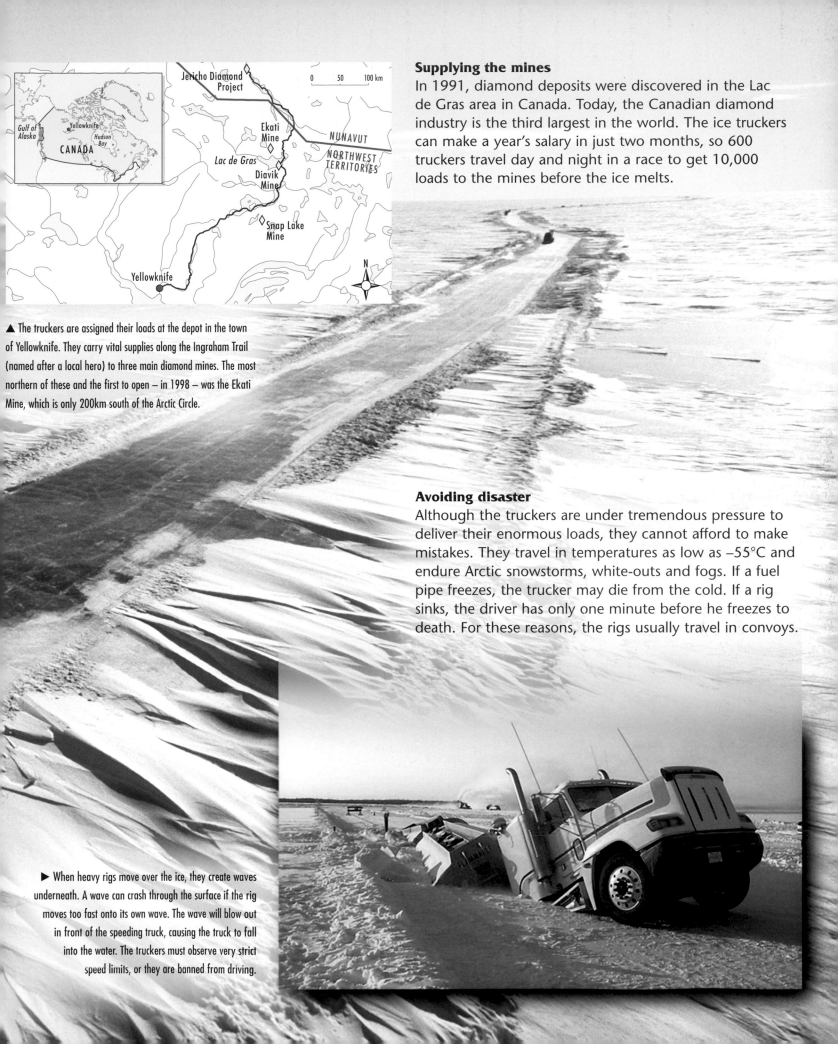

Supplying the mines

In 1991, diamond deposits were discovered in the Lac de Gras area in Canada. Today, the Canadian diamond industry is the third largest in the world. The ice truckers can make a year's salary in just two months, so 600 truckers travel day and night in a race to get 10,000 loads to the mines before the ice melts.

▲ The truckers are assigned their loads at the depot in the town of Yellowknife. They carry vital supplies along the Ingraham Trail (named after a local hero) to three main diamond mines. The most northern of these and the first to open – in 1998 – was the Ekati Mine, which is only 200km south of the Arctic Circle.

Avoiding disaster

Although the truckers are under tremendous pressure to deliver their enormous loads, they cannot afford to make mistakes. They travel in temperatures as low as –55°C and endure Arctic snowstorms, white-outs and fogs. If a fuel pipe freezes, the trucker may die from the cold. If a rig sinks, the driver has only one minute before he freezes to death. For these reasons, the rigs usually travel in convoys.

▶ When heavy rigs move over the ice, they create waves underneath. A wave can crash through the surface if the rig moves too fast onto its own wave. The wave will blow out in front of the speeding truck, causing the truck to fall into the water. The truckers must observe very strict speed limits, or they are banned from driving.

Amazing movers

Some extraordinary vehicles have been used to move about on land. Some are purpose-built to carry people over difficult terrain, while others shift the heaviest of loads. Yet others are unique – the longest car ever built was a 26-wheeled Cadillac limousine called the *American Dream* that was used mainly for films and exhibitions. It was 30.5m long and fitted out with a king-size water bed and a swimming pool complete with diving board!

▶ The Space Shuttle *Atlantis* is moved to Launch Pad 39A in September 1996. The Shuttle weighs 2,000 tonnes and the mobile launch platform 4,190 tonnes. Moving them is not an easy task. To do this, NASA has two crawler-transporters. They are the largest flatbed transporting machines in the world.

crawler weighs 2,721 tonnes

two control cabs on opposite corners allow crawler to be driven forwards or backwards without having to turn round

◄ Snowmobiles are built for endurance. They are used to travel on snow and ice, and can cross most terrains, with tracks at the rear for drive and skis up front for steering. The longest snowmobile journey was 19,574.45km in Canada and the USA. It took 60 days between January and March 2008.

Moving house

Houses, churches and even lighthouses can be shifted intact. On 5 June 1999, the 61m-tall Cape Hatteras lighthouse in North Carolina, USA, was moved inland, away from the threatening waters of the Atlantic Ocean that were getting ever nearer. The lighthouse was lifted by hydraulic jacks and steel rails placed under its base. Rollers were bolted to the rails, and five hydraulic rams pushed the load along. It took 23 days for it to travel 880m.

▼ Prefabricated buildings are often moved from place to place. In the USA, it is not unusual to see a truck moving along the highway with a two-storey house balanced behind it. Here, housing for oil workers is being carried across ice in northern Alaska.

Crawling along

Each of NASA's two crawler-transporters at the Kennedy Space Centre in Florida, USA, has 16 traction motors. The motors get their power from four generators driven by two diesel engines. The crawlers are 35m wide and 40m long. When carrying rockets and shuttles, they can only reach a maximum speed of 1.6km/h. When they travel the 5.6km from the Vehicle Assembly Building to the launch pad, it takes about six hours.

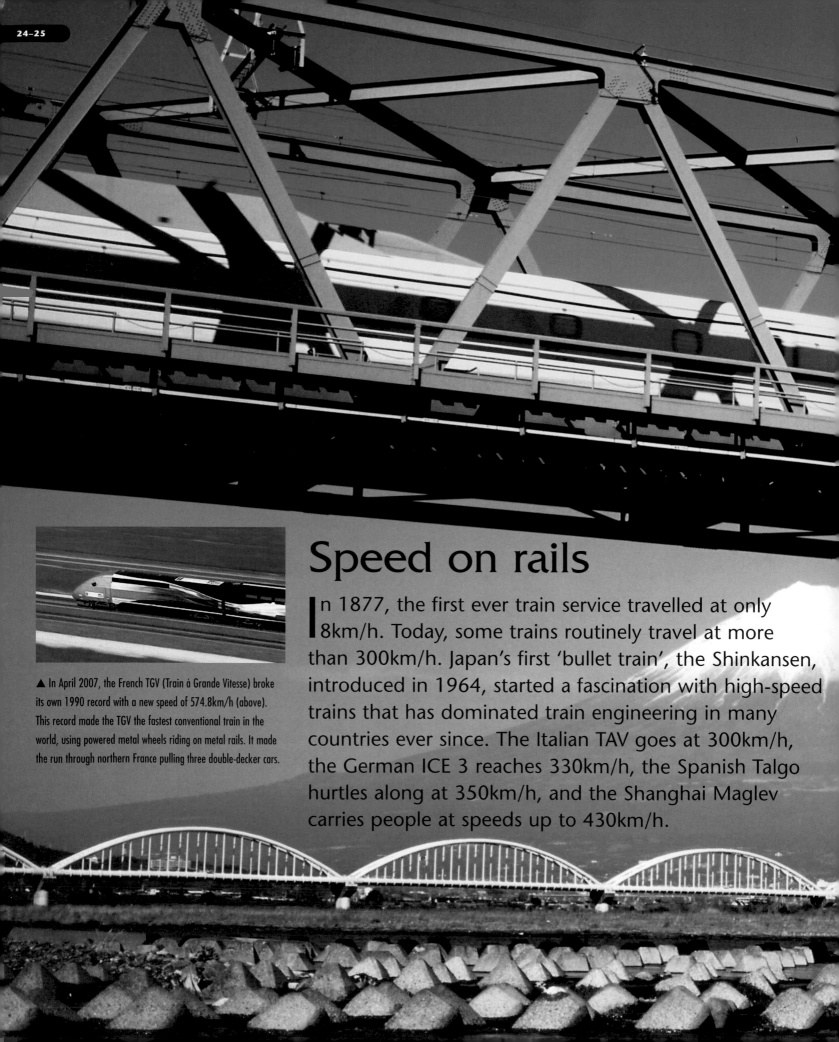

Speed on rails

In 1877, the first ever train service travelled at only 8km/h. Today, some trains routinely travel at more than 300km/h. Japan's first 'bullet train', the Shinkansen, introduced in 1964, started a fascination with high-speed trains that has dominated train engineering in many countries ever since. The Italian TAV goes at 300km/h, the German ICE 3 reaches 330km/h, the Spanish Talgo hurtles along at 350km/h, and the Shanghai Maglev carries people at speeds up to 430km/h.

▲ In April 2007, the French TGV (Train à Grande Vitesse) broke its own 1990 record with a new speed of 574.8km/h (above). This record made the TGV the fastest conventional train in the world, using powered metal wheels riding on metal rails. It made the run through northern France pulling three double-decker cars.

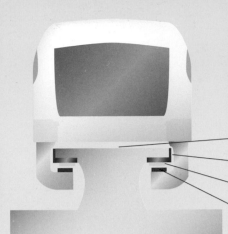

◀ The German Maglev train (left) has electromagnets on each side along its entire length. They are attracted to iron rails under the edges of the guideway that the bottom of the train wraps around. This attraction levitates the train so that it is floating about 1cm above the guideway. An electric current causes guide magnets to alternate, propelling the train along.

steel guideway

guide magnet

current in track

train electromagnet

▲ A Shinkansen train runs at an average speed of 261.8km/h along the Tokaido line with Mount Fuji in the background. 'Shinkansen' means 'new trunk line', but its popular name is *dangan ressha*, meaning 'bullet train'.

Travelling like a bullet

The super-high-speed Shinkansen travels at speeds of up to 300km/h on a network of tracks linking most of the main Japanese cities. This is the world's busiest high-speed railway network, carrying 375,000 passengers a day. Rail technology is extremely important in Japan, a country that is densely populated and looking for ways to protect the environment. The Japanese government heavily promotes rail travel and discourages the use of cars.

The new technology

The Shanghai Maglev ('magnetic levitation') train is the world's first commercial high-speed maglev, achieving a world-record speed of 501km/h. This Chinese-run train 'floats' (see above) so has no need for moving parts; it therefore needs little maintenance. It is almost silent when moving slowly, and can move very fast because there is no friction. However, maglevs cannot run on existing track, only on special tracks that are very expensive to build.

Across the roof of the world
The highest railway in the world is the line from Qinghai in China to Lhasa in Tibet, which travels across the north Tibetan plateau. The track goes through the Tanggula Pass at a dizzying height of 5,072m above sea level. More than 960km of track are higher than 4,000m, and extra oxygen is pumped into the cabins to prevent the crew and passengers suffering from altitude sickness.

Hauling freight

All over the world, freight trains are used to carry goods that people need from place to place. The trains travel on track that winds its way through the wildest of places – over high plateaux, through mountains and under seas. The freight is carried in containers, or open or covered wagons, depending on the goods and whether they need protecting from the elements. Some goods need refrigerated containers, while liquids such as petroleum or chemicals travel in tanker wagons.

▲ Higher than the Peruvian railway across the Andes, the Qinghai–Lhasa railway crosses the high Kunlun and Tanggula mountain ranges. It carries freight and passengers across 550km of permafrost. By transporting goods including minerals, agricultural products and livestock by rail instead of by road or sea, costs have been reduced by about 75 per cent.

► In remote places, where there are few railway lines, road trains are sometimes used to move bulky loads. A road train is a number of trailers pulled by one truck or heavy-duty vehicle. The longest was pulled 8km by a Kenworth C501T truck near Kalgoorlie, Australia, in 2000. It was an incredible 1,018.2m long, and made up of 79 trailers weighing a total of 1,072.3 tonnes.

Heavy goods

Some freight trains are able to move extraordinary loads. The longest freight train in the world – all 7,353km of it – travelled across western Australia on 21 June 2001. Eight diesel-electric engines moved 682 wagons, loaded with 82,262 tonnes of ore, 275km from the Newman and Yandi mines to Port Hedland. There was only one driver.

◄ In India, many trains carry both freight and passengers — and the passengers travel in or on the train in any way that they can. This train is carrying pilgrims on the way to a shrine. The Indian government runs the national rail network, which is the world's largest under one management. It transports more than two million tonnes of freight and 17 million passengers daily.

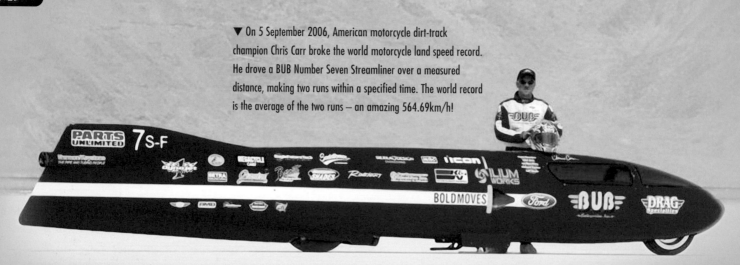

▼ On 5 September 2006, American motorcycle dirt-track champion Chris Carr broke the world motorcycle land speed record. He drove a BUB Number Seven Streamliner over a measured distance, making two runs within a specified time. The world record is the average of the two runs — an amazing 564.69km/h!

On two wheels

Races on two wheels take place on roads, racetracks, and off-road over all kinds of terrain. Bicycle races include cyclo-cross, mountain bike events, BMX races and cycle speedway on dirt tracks. One of the earliest motorcycle races was the annual Isle of Man TT (Tourist Trophy), which began in 1907. Twenty-seven competitors did ten laps of a 24km circuit on public roads. Today, as well as the TT, there are Grand Prix races and rallies, and the gruelling 24 Hours of Le Mans Moto, a yearly endurance race.

◀ Fred Rompelberg rides his record-breaking bicycle to victory on 3 October 1995 on Bonneville Salt Flats, near Salt Lake City, Utah, USA. He earned his place in history by reaching an incredible 268.831km/h, pedalling the bicycle behind a dragster to reduce wind resistance. The wheels had special lightweight aluminium rims, hubs and spokes, and the whole bike weighed only 19.5kg.

Pedal power

There are some true champions among the cyclists. Dutchman Fred Rompelberg achieved no less than 11 world records for cycling behind heavy engines, and is the holder of the Absolute Speed World Record for Cycling with a speed of nearly 270km/h (above). The American cyclist Lance Armstrong carved his name in cycling's history book as the only rider to have won the Tour de France seven times in a row (1999–2005).

The Tour de France

Probably the most difficult bicycle race of all, the Tour de France, which began in 1903, is staged over three weeks every summer. Twenty teams of nine riders each travel 3,600km across France and its neighbours, finishing in Paris. There are time trials and stages, with flat plains and high mountains to cross. Successful cyclists after each stage are rewarded with different coloured tops – yellow, green, polka-dot and white.

▲ In the 1990s, two Frenchmen, Christian Taillefer (above) and Eric Barone, battled to set a series of world records. Wearing rubber suits and aerodynamic helmets, they sped downhill on speedbikes in the French Alps. In 2007, Austrian Markus Stöckl smashed their records in the Chilean Alps with a speed of 210.4km/h.

◄ American cyclist David Zabriskie rides in a time trial during the first stage of the 2005 Tour de France race. Riders usually ride three different types of bicycle: one for time trials, one for flat road stages, and a lightweight bike for the mountainous stages. Zabriskie won this time trial, ahead of Lance Armstrong.

▲ In 1995, Emilio Scotto arrived home in Argentina at the end of the longest journey on a motorcycle. He had taken ten years to travel 735,000km, visiting many countries including China (above) on his black 1100 Honda Gold Wing, the 'Black Princess'. His book about his adventures, The Longest Ride, was published in 2007.

SUMMARY OF CHAPTER 1: LAND TRANSPORT

A fight to the finish

Between December 1898 and April 1899, the official land speed record was set and broken an amazing six times. There were only two men in the running, Camille Jenatzy of Belgium and Gaston de Chasseloup-Laubat of France. These rival racers each held the record three times, on one occasion for only a matter of hours! Camille Jenatzy was the first person to break through the speed barrier of 100km/h in his electric-powered vehicle, *La Jamais Contente* ('Never Satisfied'). On 29 April 1899, he reached 105.88km/h at Achères in France.

Salt-flat records

Bonneville Salt Flats in Utah, USA, is more than 12,000 hectares of land that is so barren that no life can exist there. It is named after the explorer Captain Benjamin Bonneville, whose employee and fur trapper Joseph Walker mapped and explored the area in the 1830s. In 1896, publisher William Randolph Hearst asked W.D. Rishel to find the shortest, fastest route for a cycle race. Rishel saw the potential for racing and in 1914, persuaded 'Terrible' Teddy Tetzlaff to try for a speed record in a car on the flats.

Tetzlaff set an unofficial record of 228.09km/h travelling across the open spaces in his Blitzen Benz. By 1949, the salt flats had become recognized as the world's premier venue for attempts on world land speed records, whether for cars, trucks, or motorcycles.

Camille Jenatzy and his wife riding in *La Jamais Contente*

Go further . . .

Discover more about racing cars and the body that governs international races, the *Fédération Internationale de l'Automobile* (FIA): www.fia.com/en-GB/Pages/HomePage.aspx

Find out all the latest news about rallies around the world from the World Rally Championship (WRC): www.wrc.com

Learn all about the Japanese 'bullet' train, the Shinkansen: http://english.jr-central.co.jp/index.html

The Kingfisher Motorsports Encyclopedia by Clive Gifford (Kingfisher, 2006)

Constructor
A person or company who supervises the building of something, such as a Formula One car.

Engineer
Someone trained and skilled in the design, construction, and use of engines and machines.

Racing driver
A person who drives a vehicle in races for a living.

Researcher
Someone who studies a subject closely so that they can present it in a detailed and accurate way.

See hundreds of vehicles from every era at: The National Motor Museum, Beaulieu, Brockenhurst, Hampshire SO42 7ZN Telephone +44 (0)1590 612 345 www.beaulieu.co.uk

Experience a day of racing at one of Britain's championship racetracks: Silverstone Circuit, Northamptonshire NN12 8TN Telephone +44 (0)844 372 8200 www.silverstone.co.uk

Find out everything about transport in a large city at: London Transport Museum, Covent Garden Piazza, London WC2E 7BB Telephone +44 (0)20 7379 6344 www.ltmuseum.co.uk

CHAPTER 2

Water transport

People who battle across oceans face some of the toughest challenges of all. They have to pit themselves against waves and tides, currents and storms, and despite months of planning may find themselves in unpredicted danger. Many of the world's greatest yacht races – the Global Challenge, the Fastnet, the Sydney to Hobart – end in disaster for some of the competitors. However, there are triumphs as well – the world's best sailors have to push themselves to their limits to circumnavigate the world on their own or bring their yacht safely into harbour ahead of the field.

There are extraordinary craft on or in the water. One of the fastest, *Miss Budweiser*, skimmed along the surface of a lake at 354km/h. Submersibles carry people to the deepest depths. And passengers travel on cruise ships that are like cities on water.

Yachts reach the first marker point at the start of the Sydney to Hobart race in December 2006.

Water speed records

▲ Donald Campbell set his final world speed record of 444.71km/h in *Bluebird K7* on 31 December 1964 on Coniston Water, UK. The last record that his father, Malcolm Campbell, had set was on the same stretch of water 25 years earlier. He reached 228.11km/h in *Bluebird K4* on 19 August 1939.

Just after 8.30am on 13 March 2004, the hydroplane *Miss Budweiser* shattered all previous world records by reaching a speed of 354.849km/h. Driven by Dave Villwock across Lake Oroville in California, USA, it set an as yet unbeaten record for propeller-driven craft. However, this is not the fastest craft on the water. That record is still held by Ken Warby's jet-powered *Spirit of Australia*, with its 511.12km/h run in 1978.

▼ *Miss Budweiser* set the record for propeller-driven craft as it sped across Lake Oroville on the return leg of its two runs. The team that built *Miss Budweiser* is probably the most successful in hydroplane racing history. Between 1963 and 2002, its boats took part in 354 races, finishing in the top three 230 times with a record 134 victories. They also designed the enclosed cockpit.

A family business

In 1964, Englishman Donald Campbell set water and land speed records in the same year, the only person ever to have done so. Between them, Donald and his father Malcolm Campbell set 11 speed records on water and 10 on land. They both drove boats and cars that they called Bluebird. Donald died on 4 January 1967 when *Bluebird K7* disintegrated at a speed in excess of 480km/h.

▲ The *Spirit of Australia* flies along on its record-breaking run on 8 October 1978. The jet-powered hydroplane reached 511.12km/h on Blowering Dam in New South Wales, Australia. It smashed its own record of 464.46km/h that had been set in November 1977.

Do-it-yourself speed

Most of the extraordinary machines that have achieved world speed records on water are designed, built and run by teams of people. However, the world's fastest speedboat, the *Spirit of Australia*, was built of balsa wood and fibreglass in the backyard of the man who set the record. Using a $69 military surplus jet engine, Ken Warby created the craft that was to make him the fastest man on water.

▲ A boat that is built purely for speed is the *Hydroptère*. This 18m-long trimaran hydrofoil, which 'flies' on water, was designed by French sailor Alain Thébault. In November 2009, *Hydroptère* broke its own world record when it travelled a nautical mile (1,852m) at an average speed of 50.17 knots (92.91km/h).

Wind power

Some of the most thrilling watersport champions use a sailboard, powered by the wind, to travel across the surface of the water. The earliest sailboards date from the late 1950s. In 1968, two Californians patented a design they called the Windsurfer, and the name stuck. Kitesurfing first became popular in Hawaii during the late 1990s. Both sports combine the skills needed for sailing and surfing. The surfers rely on the wind to help them ride the ocean's biggest waves.

Incredible journey

Flávio Jardim and Diogo Guerreiro are Brazilian windsurfing champions and expert sailors. On 17 May 2004, they set out on a journey that took them straight into the record books. Fourteen months later, on 18 July 2005, they arrived in the north of Brazil having windsurfed 8,120km along the Brazilian coast. Their expedition was sponsored by an environmental education organization.

◀ Jardim and Guerreiro's journey took them from Chui in the south of Brazil to Oiapoque in the north of the country. After five months they had reached Rio de Janiero. As they travelled along the coast, they stopped off regularly at schools and colleges to talk about topics such as renewable energy and fishing.

◀ Eco-surfers Jardim and Guerreiro were both only 23 years old when they windsurfed their way into the record books. They travelled light on their surfboards, carrying only a digital camera, a mobile phone, and a few essentials in backpacks. They completed the whole journey without a team providing support for them on land.

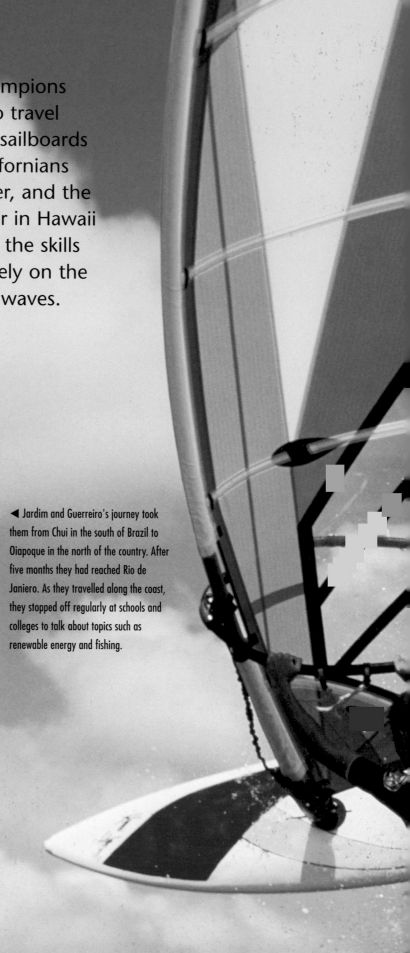

Getting up speed

A sailboard is made up of a board and a rig (a mast, boom and sail). Sails vary in shape and size and are mounted on a universal joint that allows the rig to be tilted in any direction. This means that the surfer can steer the board without a rudder. There are also wave boards and freestyle boards that are smaller and lighter. These are easier to manoeuvre, and are used to do jumps, flips and loops.

◀ A windsurfer rides a wave in Hawaii, USA. In March 2008, French windsurfer Antoine Albeau set the record for the fastest windsurf, travelling at 49.09 knots (90.91km/h) on a specially built canal at Saintes Maries de la Mer, in the south of France. The previous two records were set by Irishman Finian Maynard.

▲ In kitesurfing, a power kite pulls a rider through the water on a kiteboard. Englishwoman Andreya Wharry (above) is one of the world's best kitesurfers. She set a new world record in September 2005 – the longest continuous kitesurf. She travelled from Cornwall, southern England, to County Waterford in south-east Ireland, a distance of 213.5km, in eight hours and six minutes.

Skimming the waves

International yacht racing has produced some extraordinary sailors, but none have been more impressive than Ellen MacArthur. On 7 February 2005, she sailed her 23m trimaran *B&Q* into the record books. She had achieved the fastest solo circumnavigation of the globe. On top of that, she had broken five other records, setting speed records to the Equator, the Cape of Good Hope, Cape Leeuwin in Australia, Cape Horn and back to the Equator.

▲ Ellen MacArthur gets ready for her record-breaking trip. She completed her 44,012km journey in 71 days, 14 hours, 18 minutes and 33 seconds, beating the previous record by more than 32 hours. Astonishingly, in January 2008 her record was beaten by Frenchman Francis Joyon, who set a new time of 57 days, 13 hours, 34 minutes and six seconds in his trimaran *IDEC II*.

▲ The high-speed megayacht *Millennium 140* is powered by two powerful diesel engines and has jet turbine booster engines that allow it to reach speeds of up to 130km/h. It is the world's fastest fully equipped yacht, and can sleep ten passengers and a crew of eight. It is built with lightweight materials throughout, including a hull constructed from a special strong aluminium alloy.

Luxury travel

Megayachts are large yachts over 30m. Some megayachts are the height of luxury, but still move very fast. The world's fastest, *Millennium 140*, was designed and named for the James Bond movie *The World Is Not Enough*, in which it starred. Into this 42.4m-long yacht are packed a skylounge deck, grand salon, formal dining room, country kitchen, and master suite complete with jacuzzi.

Competitive streak

Yacht racing involves a great variety of sailing boats, from dinghies to giant ocean racers. It is either inshore or offshore. Inshore usually takes place within sight of land or from land to nearby islands. Offshore racing goes across open water and oceans, and includes some of the most exciting and challenging races in the world – the Fastnet, Sydney to Hobart, Global Challenge and Transpacific.

◀ The Australian yacht *Brindabella* takes part in the 59th Sydney to Hobart yacht race in December 2003. This annual 'Bluewater Classic' race began in 1945 with only nine runners. In the last decade there have been anything up to 371 competitors. The fastest race was run in one day, 18 hours, 40 minutes and 10 seconds by *Wild Oats XI* in 2005.

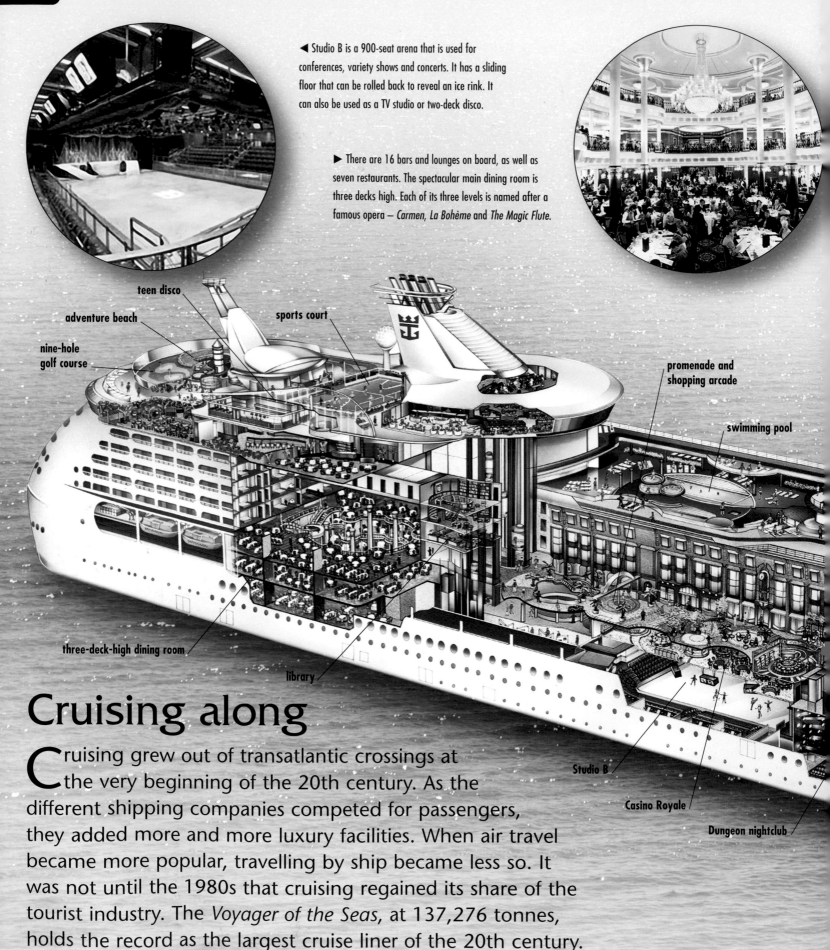

◀ Studio B is a 900-seat arena that is used for conferences, variety shows and concerts. It has a sliding floor that can be rolled back to reveal an ice rink. It can also be used as a TV studio or two-deck disco.

▶ There are 16 bars and lounges on board, as well as seven restaurants. The spectacular main dining room is three decks high. Each of its three levels is named after a famous opera – *Carmen*, *La Bohème* and *The Magic Flute*.

teen disco

adventure beach

sports court

nine-hole golf course

promenade and shopping arcade

swimming pool

three-deck-high dining room

library

Studio B

Casino Royale

Dungeon nightclub

Cruising along

Cruising grew out of transatlantic crossings at the very beginning of the 20th century. As the different shipping companies competed for passengers, they added more and more luxury facilities. When air travel became more popular, travelling by ship became less so. It was not until the 1980s that cruising regained its share of the tourist industry. The *Voyager of the Seas*, at 137,276 tonnes, holds the record as the largest cruise liner of the 20th century.

First of its kind

When it was launched in 1999, the *Voyager of the Seas* was revolutionary both for its engineering and the amazing variety of onboard activities it offered. It can carry up to 3,838 passengers and 1,181 crew. At 310.9m, it is nearly as long as three football fields. It is 47.55m wide and its 14 decks rise more than 61m above the waterline. Other ships built by Royal Caribbean since are larger still.

Floating resort

On this luxury liner, passengers are able to enjoy the first rock-climbing wall at sea, as well as a golf course and driving range, a basketball court and an in-line skating track. There are swimming pools, whirlpools, a spa and a large health and fitness centre. There is even special provision for the crew, who have their own deck complete with whirlpools, a gym, dining rooms and a disco.

► Right down the centre of the ship runs the Royal Promenade, a winding street four decks high. At two places along its length, there are atria (halls) that rise 11 decks above the passengers' heads. The promenade is a shopping mall with shops, clubs, cafes and bars.

▼ In the evenings, there is entertainment to suit all tastes. The Scala Theatre (below) is five decks high and seats 1,350 people. It has a hydraulic orchestra pit and stage area, which can be raised and lowered. There is gaming in the Casino Royale, as well as a disco, jazz club and nightclub.

observation point

observation deck

fitness centre and spa

theatre

Across the seas

There have been many incredible journeys across the seas. On 13 May 1958, Ben Carlin, an Australian, arrived in Montreal, Canada. He had taken eight years to circumnavigate the world in an amphibious jeep. He travelled 17,800km across water and 62,800km across land. When he set off in July 1950, he expected to travel across the Atlantic Ocean in only nine or ten days. Instead, it took 23 days because of a hurricane!

▲ Ben Carlin's jeep was called *Half-Safe*, and was a modified ex-World War II vehicle. He began the journey with his new wife, Elinore, but she suffered from seasickness. When they reached India, she decided to jump ship, and he had a series of other shipmates for the rest of the voyage.

salt-water resistant interior

zero emissions, so will not pollute

car is open underwater so exit is easy in an emergency

driver and passenger breathe compressed air from fitted tank

▲ The *sQuba* submarine car has three electric motors powered by rechargeable lithium-ion batteries. One of the motors powers the back wheels on land. The other two power the propellers in the stern to push the car along underwater. The *sQuba* dives to 10m below the surface and can stay underwater for up to two hours.

► On 7 December 2007, in Sydney Harbour, a 6.1-m *Sealegs* craft became the fastest amphibious vehicle over 500m on water, travelling the distance in just 18 seconds. Two years before, in 2005, *Sealegs* almost halved the record time for the fastest crossing of the English Channel set by an *Aquada* driven by Richard Branson.

hydraulics raise and lower the wheels front and back for land use

Driving underwater

Fifty years after *Half-Safe* completed its historic journey, another amphibious car hit the headlines. The first underwater car in the world, the *sQuba* can be driven both on land and underwater. Like the imaginary car driven by James Bond in *The Spy Who Loved Me* (1977), it is made from a Lotus. It travels at up to 120km/h on land, 6km/h on water, and 3km/h below the surface.

body panels are made of lightweight hi-tech materials

Saving the Earth

Travelling on or in water is always a great challenge and has inspired some revolutionary designs. One craft went faster by actually submarining through the crests of the waves with its wave-piercing Kevlar hull. *Earthrace* (below), built with environmentally friendly materials, was carbon neutral and even had on-board recycling. It completed a record-breaking circumnavigation of the globe fuelled with 100 per cent renewable biodiesel.

► The futuristic trimaran *Earthrace* set out on its journey on 27 April 2008 from Sagunto in Spain, arriving back there on 27 June. It had taken 60 days, 23 hours and 49 minutes, and knocked nearly 14 days off the previous record set by *Ocean 7 Adventurer* in 1998.

Exploring the depths

Submersibles are small, but very manoeuvrable. They are usually tethered to a support vessel and so have a relatively short range. They can be used to explore places that are normally impossible to reach. When the wreck of the *Titanic* was discovered on 1 September 1985, it was at a depth of 3,800m off the coast of Newfoundland. A year later, a manned deep-sea submersible called *Alvin* and an ROV (remotely operated vehicle) named *Jason Junior* were used to explore the wreck.

Scientific explorer

Built in 1964, the US Navy's Deep Submergence Vehicle *Alvin* was the world's first deep-ocean submersible able to carry passengers. The pressure hull of the cockpit, which holds a team of three, is made of strong titanium. The life-support system can keep them alive for up to 72 hours if necessary. *Alvin* has been used to find hydrothermal vents and has helped to find at least 300 new animal species.

▲ *Aluminaut* was the world's first submersible built out of aluminium. A deep-sea research vehicle, it helped to recover *Alvin* from the Atlantic Ocean in 1969. The smaller submersible had become lost in 1968 when a cable snapped. The crew of three managed to escape, but *Alvin* sank in 1,500m of water. A year later, the crew of *Aluminaut* managed to secure a line on *Alvin*, and the passenger-carrying robot was hauled up to the surface.

▼ *Alvin* may be the world's oldest research submersible, but it has been modified and updated several times. It can go as deep as 4,500m during dives of 6 to 10 hours. Its six reversible thrusters allow it to manoeuvre or hover in one place. It is equipped with still and video cameras, and has robotic arms to manipulate tools or collect samples.

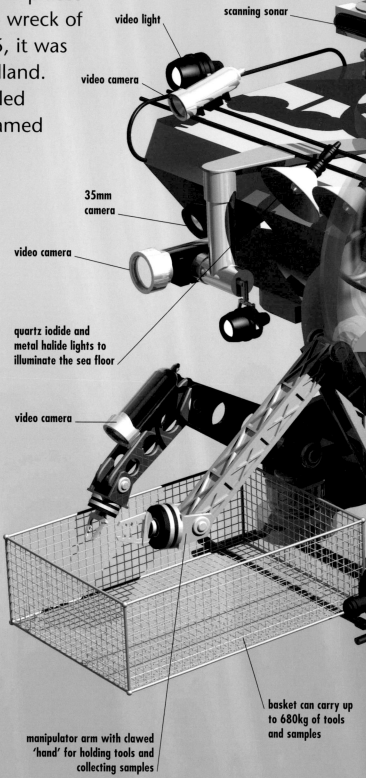

scanning sonar

video light

video camera

35mm camera

video camera

quartz iodide and metal halide lights to illuminate the sea floor

video camera

manipulator arm with clawed 'hand' for holding tools and collecting samples

basket can carry up to 680kg of tools and samples

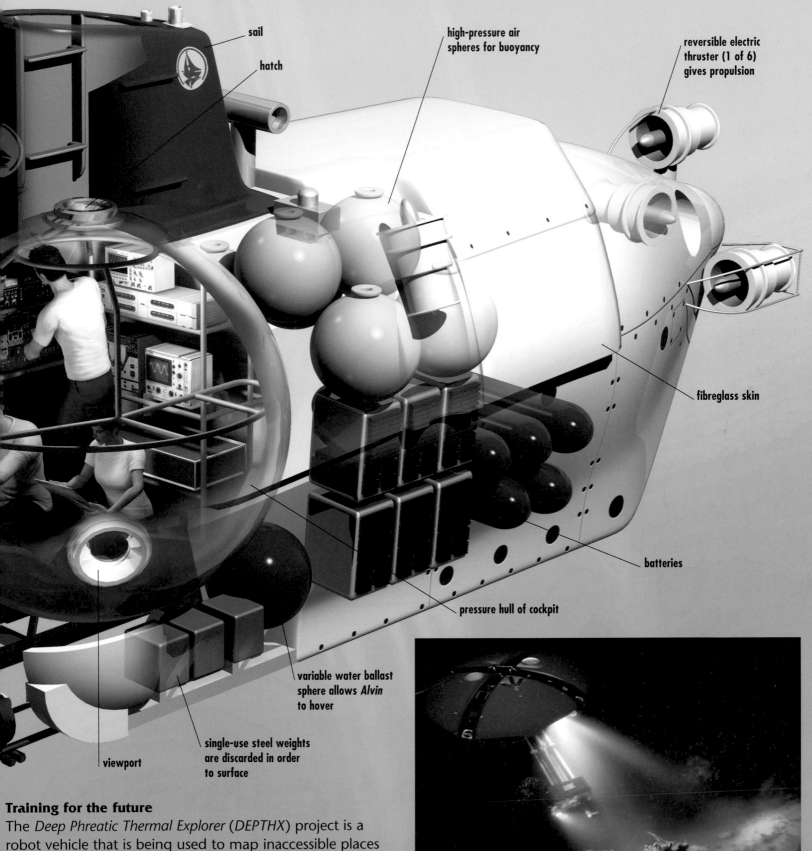

sail

hatch

high-pressure air
spheres for buoyancy

reversible electric
thruster (1 of 6)
gives propulsion

fibreglass skin

batteries

pressure hull of cockpit

variable water ballast
sphere allows *Alvin*
to hover

single-use steel weights
are discarded in order
to surface

viewport

Training for the future

The *Deep Phreatic Thermal Explorer* (*DEPTHX*) project is a robot vehicle that is being used to map inaccessible places such as deep, flooded caverns. In May 2007, it reached the bottom of the world's deepest sinkhole, El Zacatón in Mexico. The NASA-funded robot is designed to explore for life in the Earth's extreme regions, and maybe in the future on Jupiter's ice-covered moon, Europa.

▲ *DEPTHX* is 2.5m in diameter and weighs 1,500kg. The robot is equipped with SLAM (simultaneous localization and mapping) technology with which it created 3D maps of El Zacatón's interior. On the way down the sinkhole, *DEPTHX* collected samples of water and materiuls from the walls. It discovered the previously unexplored bottom of the sinkhole, 318m below the surface.

SUMMARY OF CHAPTER 2: WATER TRANSPORT

Crossing the Atlantic

In 1838, the steamship *SS Sirius* travelled from Cork in Ireland to Sandy Hook in New Jersey, USA, in 18 days, four hours and 22 minutes. This marked the beginning of ships competing to cross the Atlantic Ocean in the fastest time. In the 1860s, the transatlantic shipping companies created the Blue Riband prize. To begin with, the winners flew a blue pennant from the mast. Later, in 1935, a trophy was introduced. The prize is awarded for average speed during the journey, and there are separate prizes for eastward and westward crossings. Cunard's *Queen Mary* twice held the Blue Riband for crossing the ocean in both directions, in 1936 and 1938, and held this record until 1952.

The ships of tomorrow

People have always explored their world in boats, and boat building has progressed dramatically over the centuries. Prehistoric coracles were made out of animal skins stretched around a wood frame, and ancient rafts were constructed from bundles of reeds. Today's ships are built for purpose, whether they are sleek fibreglass racing yachts, steel-hulled battleships or multi-hulled trimarans. In the future, new hull designs and efficient propulsion systems will enable sailors to go further, and in quicker times, than ever before.

Tugboats guide the *Queen Mary* into the 51st Street Pier, New York City, USA

Go further...

Discover everything about the sea and ships by visiting the National Maritime Museum
www.nmm.ac.uk/server/show/nav.3560

Find out the latest yachting news: www.rya.org.uk/newsevents/Pages/default.aspx

Learn all about *Alvin* and other submersibles: http://oceanexplorer.noaa.gov/technology/subs/subs.html

The New Complete Sailing Manual by Steve Sleight (Dorling Kindersley, 2005)

Windsurfing by Peter Hart (The Crowood Press Ltd, 2005)

Designer
Someone who creates plans for use in making something, such as a ship.

Explorer
A person who travels into little-known regions to find out more about them.

Kitesurfer
A rider on a surfboard who is pulled through the water by a large kite.

Sailor
A person who works on a ship; any member of a ship's crew.

Windsurfer
Someone who rides on water, using a special surfboard that has a sail.

Find out about Britain and the sea through the ages at: The National Maritime Museum, Greenwich, London SE10 9NF
Telephone +44 (0)20 8858 4422
www.nmm.ac.uk

Explore the world of windsurfing with the UK Windsurfing Association: UKWA, PO Box 703, Haywards Heath RH16 9EE
Email admin@ukwindsurfing.com
http://ukwindsurfing.com

Try some water sports yourself at: National Water Sports Centre, Adbolton Lane, Home Pierrepont, Nottingham NG12 2LU
Telephone +44 (0)115 982 1212
www.nwscnotts.com

CHAPTER 3

Air transport

Travelling through the Earth's atmosphere is exhilarating. Balloons and airships float along, their canopies filled with low-density gas. Glider pilots search for thermals to lift them, silently spiralling ever higher. Airliners travel at 10,000m, carrying people from one side of the world to the other in less than a day. And paragliding, hang-gliding and freefall parachuting are exciting sports for those who want to feel as if they are really flying like the birds.

The fastest way for anyone to travel is by air, and the speediest planes are jets that travel several times faster than the speed of sound. The fastest aircraft of all was an unmanned experimental NASA aircraft that, on 16 November 2004, reached almost Mach 10 – ten times the speed of sound! In the future, this aerial technology may develop so that people are able to fly through space to the Moon or to nearby planets on regular scheduled flights.

The unpiloted X-43A scramjet-powered research aircraft travelled at Mach 9.6 (11,760km/h) to set a world speed record.

Fastest in the air

The birth of the jet engine in the late 1930s changed aviation forever. Over the following decades, new engine designs made it possible to travel at ever-increasing speeds. The fastest aircraft of all are supersonic, travelling faster than the speed of sound. They are mostly high altitude, highly manoeuvrable reconnaissance aircraft. The only supersonic passenger plane was Concorde, which had a cruising speed of Mach 2.04 (2,200km/h).

▶ The United States Air Force *SR-71 Blackbird* reconnaissance jet, built in the mid-1960s, remains the fastest manned jet with a speed more than three times the speed of sound. The supersonic jet's titanium skin resisted the heat generated at this speed and protected the aluminium frame underneath. With side-looking radar and the ability to survey an area of 260,000km², the extraordinary plane was also capable of avoiding missiles.

▲ The fastest combat jet is the Russian MiG-25 fighter, designed in the 1960s for high-altitude flight. It has been tracked travelling at about Mach 3.2 (3,395km/h). The MiG-25 set ten records while it was being tested, including speed over a 500km circuit, absolute altitude, and time to climb to an altitude of 30,000m.

Speeding in secrecy
Records for speed in the air are hard to establish. Usually, the jets concerned are developed for military use, so their speeds are not published. The world speed record is held by a MiG-25 (above), which was recorded by US radar flying over Israel at Mach 3.2 (3,395km/h) in 1973. The speed destroyed the engines and since then these planes could travel safely at up to only Mach 2.83 (3,000km/h).

► The *Martin XP6M-1 SeaMaster*, which first flew in 1955, was the fastest flying boat ever built, with a top speed of 965km/h. This US Navy aircraft had an all-metal hull with sharply swept-back wings. Its four turbojet engines were set on top of the wings to prevent them from being damaged by the water.

Flight of the *Blackbird*

From its first flight in 1964, the *SR-71 Blackbird* jet ruled the skies, flying top-secret missions for nearly 25 years. It still holds the record as the fastest aircraft of all, with a top speed of Mach 3.3 (3,529.56km/h). On its last flight on 6 March 1990, it set a record flying from Los Angeles to Washington D.C. in one hour, four minutes and two seconds at an average speed of 3,452km/h.

The largest loads

The largest aircraft carry the largest loads, whether passengers or cargo. Often airliners are designed for either use – for example, the largest passenger airliner in the world, the Airbus A380, can also be set up to carry only cargo. Although the A380 carries the most passengers, it is not the largest and heaviest aircraft of all. That is the Ukrainian An-225 *Cossack*, designed to carry the Soviet space shuttle in 1988. It has a wingspan of 88.4m and is 84m long.

high-pressure hydraulic system to move rudders uses a pump that weighs 20 per cent less than on other similar aircraft

◄ A Super Puma heavy-lift helicopter is unloaded from an Airbus A300-600 Super Transporter. The helicopter is 16.3m in length and 4.6m tall, and the Airbus has the capacity to carry two fully assembled helicopters with blades folded. Cargo is lifted out through the upwards-hinging main cargo door.

baggage containers in cargo hold on lower deck

economy-class seating on main deck

wingspan of 79.8m

leading-edge flaps

dampeners on Rolls-Royce engines mean noise is half that of other jumbo jets

Super loaded
The Airbus A300-600 Super Transporter, nicknamed 'Beluga', is one of the world's largest cargo carriers. Launched in 1994, it has the same wings, lower fuselage, undercarriage and cockpit as the A300-600 passenger plane. The difference is that it is two storeys high, almost twice as long as a basketball court, and able to transport up to 47 tonnes of cargo. It is used mainly to carry large aircraft parts, or even whole aircraft and helicopters.

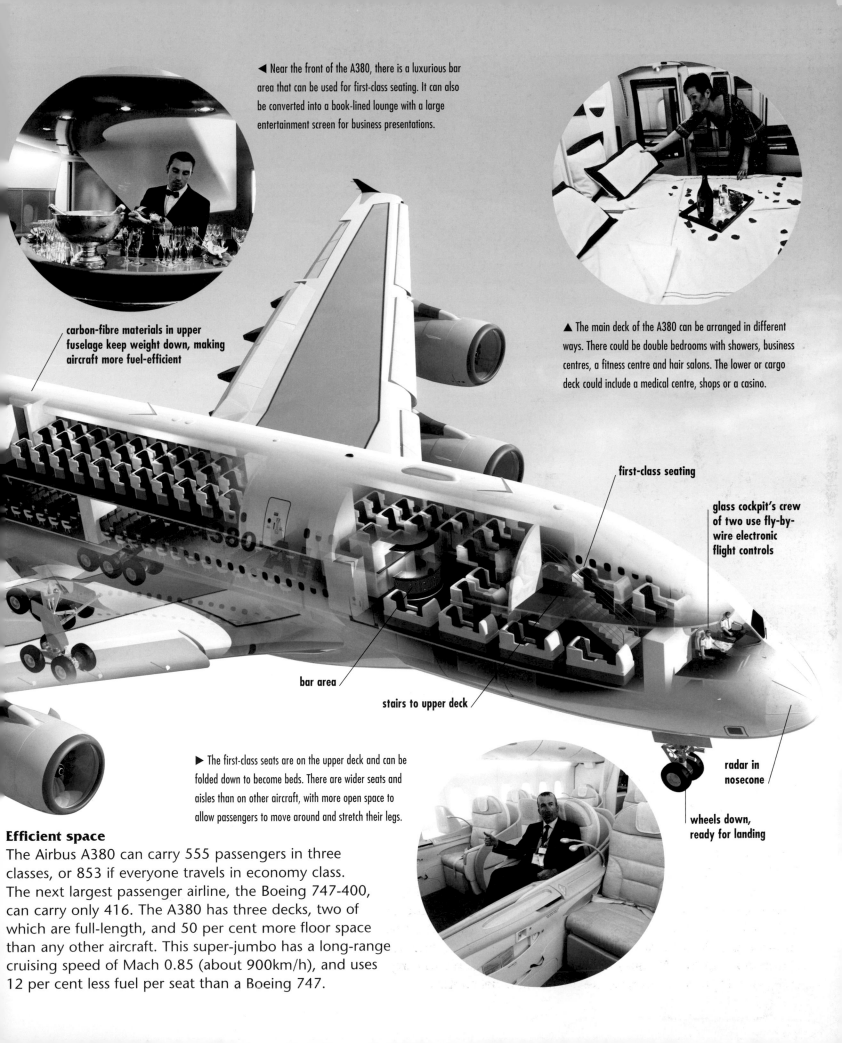

◄ Near the front of the A380, there is a luxurious bar area that can be used for first-class seating. It can also be converted into a book-lined lounge with a large entertainment screen for business presentations.

carbon-fibre materials in upper fuselage keep weight down, making aircraft more fuel-efficient

▲ The main deck of the A380 can be arranged in different ways. There could be double bedrooms with showers, business centres, a fitness centre and hair salons. The lower or cargo deck could include a medical centre, shops or a casino.

first-class seating

glass cockpit's crew of two use fly-by-wire electronic flight controls

bar area

stairs to upper deck

radar in nosecone

▶ The first-class seats are on the upper deck and can be folded down to become beds. There are wider seats and aisles than on other aircraft, with more open space to allow passengers to move around and stretch their legs.

wheels down, ready for landing

Efficient space

The Airbus A380 can carry 555 passengers in three classes, or 853 if everyone travels in economy class. The next largest passenger airline, the Boeing 747-400, can carry only 416. The A380 has three decks, two of which are full-length, and 50 per cent more floor space than any other aircraft. This super-jumbo has a long-range cruising speed of Mach 0.85 (about 900km/h), and uses 12 per cent less fuel per seat than a Boeing 747.

▼ The longest journey made by a powered paraglider was that of American Bob Holloway in 2004. Between 18 June and 12 July, he travelled 4,150km from Astoria, Oregon, to Washington, Missouri, following the trail of early 19th-century explorers Meriwether Lewis and William Clark. Like them, he travelled from one side of the North American continent to the other.

Hanging in the air

Gliding takes many forms. In hang-gliding, the pilot lies facing downwards in a harness hanging from a lightweight metal V-shaped framework that supports a fabric wing. Paragliders sit in a harness that also hangs from a fabric wing. However, the wing's crescent shape is formed only by the pressure of air entering through vents at the front.

Gliding and paragliding

In 852, inventor Abbas Ibn Firnas jumped from the minaret of a mosque in Córdoba, Spain. He survived because he used a large cloak like a parachute. Inspired, he built a glider that he tried to fly from the nearby Mount of the Bride. Unfortunately he crashed, but over the following centuries, many others tried to follow his lead. Ibn Firnas controlled his glider by shifting his body, just like the pilots do in modern hang-gliders.

▲ Paragliders launch themselves by running either over a cliff or down a slope. They can travel great distances. In July 2006, Aljaz Valic of Slovenia achieved the 'out-and-return' world record of 259.7km in Slovenia. In December 2008, South African pilot Nevil Hulett flew 502.9km to gain the world straight-distance record in Copperton, South Africa.

Flying high

Gliders can stay aloft for hours. They find the updrafts of warm air from the Earth's surface called thermals, and circle in them at altitudes of up to 3,000m. They also use ridge lift, when wind blows against the face of a hill and is forced upwards. Wave lift – waves in the atmosphere that are like ripples on water – helped lift Steve Fossett and Einar Enevoldson into the stratosphere and set the world glider altitude record of 15,447m in Argentina in 2006.

▲ On 19 December 2007, Laszlo Hegedus of Hungary set a world speed record over a triangular course. He flew 1,250km at an average speed of 151.5km/h at Bitterwasser in Namibia. His glider was the elegant Schempp-Hirth Nimbus 4T (above). Pamela Kurstjens-Hawkins of the UK holds three speed and three distance gliding world records, all achieved when flying a Nimbus 4T.

Highest, longest, furthest

At 8.05am on Monday 1 March 1999, *Breitling Orbiter 3* took off from the grounds of Château d'Oex in the Swiss Alps. On 21 March, it touched down in the Egyptian desert, after it had completed the first successful non-stop circumnavigation of the world by balloon. On board were the pilots Bertrand Piccard and Brian Jones. They had travelled 45,755km in a flight lasting 19 days, 21 hours and 55 minutes.

▲ Swiss psychiatrist and balloonist Bertrand Piccard waves to the 5,000-strong crowd that gathered to see off the *Breitling Orbiter 3*. Balloonist Brian Jones, from England, was his co-pilot on this history-making flight. Piccard had failed with his first two attempts in *Orbiter* in 1997 and *Orbiter 2* in 1998.

◄ Satellite-based systems in the forward cockpit of the gondola were used to communicate with the control team on the ground. The control team used two GPS systems to track the balloon's route in real time, and calculate the best altitude for the pilots to fly at.

Up, up and away

Piccard and Jones broke distance, time and endurance world records with this flight. For nearly three weeks, they travelled at altitudes of up to 11,373m and were driven by jet-stream winds at speeds of up to 300km/h. At one point, Piccard climbed out of the gondola to chip icicles off the balloon with a pickaxe! Along the sides of the gondola that hung underneath *Breitling Orbiter 3* were 32 titanium cylinders that fuelled the balloon's six burners.

Living space

The gondola in which the two men travelled was 5.4m long and made of a mixture of Kevlar and carbon fibre material. Solar panels under the gondola recharged batteries on board to provide electrical power, and burners kept the temperature at a constant 15°C for most of the time. There was one bunk in the centre and a cleverly designed pressure-operated toilet at the rear. The two men lived mainly on rehydrated meals. They followed a strict rotation of eight hours at the controls, eight hours working with one another, and eight hours sleeping in the bunk.

◄ When fully inflated, the balloon was 55m tall. It was made of a nylon fabric welded to a special helium-tight membrane. This in turn was covered in a skin coated with aluminium to give good temperature control. The gondola was 3.1m high and weighed 2,000kg.

Strange but true

During the last 100 years, some of the most extraordinary flying machines have been built. Some have been so huge that it is a wonder that they were able to stay aloft. Others have set, broken and held records for more than half a century. Flying boats and airships, used for transport, have been at the centre of great success and dire disaster. Also, people have tested their own abilities to the limit in the effort to develop new ways to fly.

Winged wonder

On 2 November 1947, the *Hughes H-4 Hercules*, the largest flying boat ever built, made its first and only flight. Named the 'Spruce Goose' by its critics, it was 66.6m long and held the record as the largest plane in the world for many years. It still holds the record for the longest wingspan at 97.54m. The *H-4 Hercules* was built entirely of wood by a team of engineers led by eccentric American multi-millionaire Howard Hughes.

▼ With Howard Hughes at the controls, the Spruce Goose glided over a 5km stretch of water at Long Beach, California. It reached 145km/h but only achieved an altitude of 21m for one minute. Afterwards, Hughes had the flying boat put in a hangar and kept in good flying condition until he died in 1976.

Gas-filled giants

For many years, the German-built zeppelin airships ruled the skies. A zeppelin had a rigid internal metal skeleton that contained gas-filled bags which gave the craft lift. Built into the base was a compartment for the passengers and crew. When the *Hindenburg* was launched in March 1936, it was the largest airship ever built. It was 245m long, and had a maximum speed of 135km/h.

◄ At 7.25pm on 6 May 1937, the *Hindenburg* burst into flames as it came in to land at Lakehurst, New Jersey, USA. A spark caused the rear section of the hydrogen-filled zeppelin to catch fire as the airship was being secured to a mooring tower. In only 37 seconds, the airship was completely destroyed. Despite the intensity of the flames, 62 of the 97 passengers and crew on board survived.

▲ The *LZ-127 Graf Zeppelin* flies over London in 1931. The airship operated from 1928 to 1937; during this time it flew 590 flights and more than 1.5 million km. In 1929, while circumnavigating the globe, the *Graf Zeppelin* crossed from Japan to San Francisco, USA — the first non-stop flight of any aircraft across the Pacific Ocean.

▶ On 16 August 1960, wearing a pressurized suit, American Joseph Kittinger jumped out of the gondola of a helium balloon, *Excelsior III*, at 31,333m. His records for the highest balloon ascent, the highest parachute jump, the longest parachute freefall (four minutes and 36 seconds), and the fastest speed by a human through the atmosphere (up to 988km/h) still stand.

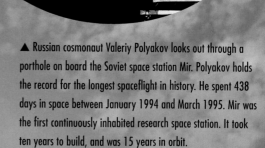
▲ The ATV *Jules Verne*, launched in March 2008, was a 20.7-tonne cargo ship designed by the European Space Agency (ESA). It delivered 6.6 tonnes of cargo, including food, water, oxygen and spare parts, to the International Space Station (ISS). In September, after carrying away 6.4 tonnes of waste, the craft underwent controlled destruction as it re-entered Earth's atmosphere. *Jules Verne* was the first of a fleet of ATVs, all capable of boosting the ISS into a higher orbit.

Into space

Carrying cargo and passengers into space is big business in more senses than one. The vehicles used are probably the most expensive built on Earth, and they carry some of the largest loads. These transporters have included the Russian Progress M-53 freighter, the Space Shuttle orbiters, and the Automated Transfer Vehicle (ATV). They have carried materials to build space stations, and supplies and fuel for crews who stay on them. They have also launched satellites and brought them back to Earth.

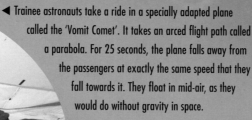

◄ Trainee astronauts take a ride in a specially adapted plane called the 'Vomit Comet'. It takes an arced flight path called a parabola. For 25 seconds, the plane falls away from the passengers at exactly the same speed that they fall towards it. They float in mid-air, as they would do without gravity in space.

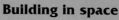
▲ Russian cosmonaut Valeriy Polyakov looks out through a porthole on board the Soviet space station Mir. Polyakov holds the record for the longest spaceflight in history. He spent 438 days in space between January 1994 and March 1995. Mir was the first continuously inhabited research space station. It took ten years to build, and was 15 years in orbit.

Building in space

The construction of the ISS (International Space Station) began in 1998, and it is still being assembled 350km above the Earth's surface. It travels at an average speed of 7.7km/sec, and orbits the Earth 15.75 times per day. The space station is a joint project by the space agencies of the USA, Russia, Japan, Canada and Europe. Materials to build the ISS are carried up into space by shuttles and the ATV.

Shuttle service

There are currently three space shuttles in the NASA fleet – *Atlantic*, *Endeavour* and *Discovery*. There were originally five, but *Challenger* disintegrated 73 seconds after launch in 1986, while *Columbia* broke apart during re-entry into Earth's atmosphere in 2003. The shuttles look like aircraft with their double-delta wings, and carry astronauts and payloads to satellites and space stations. They are launched as rockets into orbit round the Earth, and land like gliders after re-entry.

▼ The Space Shuttle *Discovery* approaches the ISS to dock. This shuttle has flown more flights than any other spacecraft. Like the other shuttles, it has a large payload bay (4.6m by 18.3m), from which in April 1990 it launched the Hubble Space Telescope.

SUMMARY OF CHAPTER 3: AIR TRANSPORT

Reaching the skies

Over the centuries, many people have tried to fly. In 1783, the French Montgolfier brothers filled a huge paper balloon with hot air and it rose into the air carrying two men. Nearly a century later Henri Giffard invented the first dirigible, or steerable balloon. In 1853, Sir George Cayley built a full-size glider which is said to have carried his coachman across a valley. But it was in December 1903, at Kitty Hawk in the USA, that Orville and Wilbur Wright flew their petrol-engined flying machine, the Flyer, for 40m. Real air travel had begun.

Transatlantic triumph

In April 1913, the UK's *Daily Mail* newspaper offered a prize of £10,000 to the first person to make a non-stop flight from North America to Great Britain or Ireland. Two months later, on 14 June, British fliers John Alcock and Arthur Whitten Brown took off from Lester's Field in St John's, Newfoundland (now part of Canada), in a twin-engined Vickers Vimy IV. Alcock piloted and Brown navigated, and despite engine trouble and bad weather – at one point snow filled the cockpit – they landed at Clifden, in western Ireland. Thinking they had chosen a green field for their landing, they actually came down in a bog on Derrygimla Moor. They had travelled 3,040km in just over 16 hours and were the first people to fly non-stop across the Atlantic.

Alcock and Brown's landing damaged the aircraft but they were not hurt.

Go further...

Find out about learning to hang-glide or paraglide from the British Hang Gliding and Paragliding Association: www.bhpa.co.uk/

Explore the history of flight at the National Museums of Scotland site: www.nms.ac.uk/museumofflight homepage.aspx

Discover where to see air shows in the UK on Flightline UK: www.airshows.org.uk/

Flying Machine by Andrew Nahum (Dorling Kindersley, 2004)

Ultimate Thrill Sports: Hang Gliding by Noel Whittall (Gareth Stevens Publishing, 2007)

Balloonist
Someone who flies or rides in a balloon as a sport or hobby.

Cosmonaut
A Russian or Soviet astronaut, a person trained to travel in a spacecraft.

Inventor
The first person to think of or make something.

Paraglider
Someone who travels from a height through the air wearing a wide, steerable parachute.

Pilot
A person qualified to fly a plane, balloon or other aircraft.

See an air display and the American Air Museum at Duxford aviation museum: Imperial War Museum Duxford, Cambridgeshire CB22 4QR Telephone +44 (0)1223 835000 http://duxford.iwm.org.uk

For a large aircraft collection visit: Fleet Air Arm Museum, RNAS Yeovilton, near Ilchester, Somerset BA22 8HT Telephone +44 (0)1935 840 565 www.fleetairarm.com

Visit the Science Museum and learn all about flight and space transport: Science Museum, Exhibition Road, South Kensington, London SW7 2DD Telephone +44 (0)870 870 4868 www.sciencemuseum.org.uk

Glossary

acceleration
The rate of increase in the speed of a moving object.

air resistance
The force that resists the movement of an object through the air.

alloy
A mixture of two or more metals, or a mixture of a metal and a non-metal.

altitude
The height of an object above sea level or above the Earth's surface.

amphibious
Something (e.g. a vehicle) capable of operating on both land and water.

biodiesel
Vegetable oil and animal fat that is converted into fuel for heating systems and diesel engines.

carbon fibre
A strong, lightweight material made of almost pure carbon, used in the construction of aircraft and spacecraft.

carbon neutral
Giving off zero carbon dioxide into the atmosphere. Something is carbon neutral if either it gives off no carbon dioxide at all or if it gives off no more carbon dioxide than it absorbs.

centrifuge
A machine that spins round at high speed, used to test the affects of acceleration and deceleration on astronauts and pilots.

circumnavigation
To go completely around something, for example the Earth.

cosmonaut
A Russian or Soviet who is trained to take part in the flight of a spacecraft.

cyclo-cross
A bicycle race over a cross-country course, which can require the rider to carry the bicycle over obstacles.

deceleration
A decrease in the speed of something.

density
A measure of how tightly packed the mass is in a substance.

double delta
The wing of an aircraft in the form of two triangles.

downforce
The downward pressure created by a car that allows it to travel faster by improving grip on the track or road.

drag
The force that slows an object down as it travels through a liquid or gas.

drag racing
A race between cars to find out which can accelerate fastest from a standstill.

dragster
A car specially built or modified for drag racing.

emissions
Substances discharged into the air from an engine.

endurance
The ability to continue or last.

excavator
A machine used for digging and moving soil, sand or gravel.

Two trucks move a family home in the USA.

fibreglass
A plastic material reinforced with fine, threadlike pieces of glass.

flatbed
A truck or trailer that has an open back with no sides, and is used to carry large objects.

fly-by-wire
A semi-automatic, computerized flight control used for flying aircraft or spacecraft.

freefall
Describes the initial fall through the air by parachutists before they deploy their parachute.

freight
Goods or cargo carried from place to place by water, land or air.

fuselage
The central part of an aircraft, to which the wings and tail are attached.

g-force
The force acting on a body as a result of acceleration or gravity.

geothermal
Describes the energy harnessed from hot rocks inside the Earth.

hydraulic
Describes a machine that is made to operate by a fluid under pressure.

hydrofoil
A speedboat that has winglike structures attached to its hull, which lift it so that it skims over the water at high speed.

hydroplane
A high-powered boat designed to travel along the surface of the water at high speed.

hydrothermal vent
An opening in the sea-floor from which hot, mineral-rich water flows.

SR-71 Blackbird

Francis Joyon's trimaran, *IDEC II,* in which he beat Ellen MacArthur's solo round-the-world record in January 2008.

jet engine
An engine that produces a stream of hot gas that propels a vehicle forwards.

jet stream
Strong winds that circle the Earth about 10km above the surface.

Kevlar
A lightweight but very strong material used for many goods including tyres, ropes and sails.

lift
The upward force, produced by wings, that keeps an aircraft in the air.

Mach
A measurement of speed in relation to the speed of sound. Mach 1 is the same as the speed of sound. The speed of sound is around 1,200km/h at sea level, but it varies with the temperature, humidity and pressure of air.

orbiter
A spacecraft, planet or satellite that orbits another body, such as the Earth.

permafrost
Ground that is permanently frozen.

prefabricated
Manufactured in sections for quick assembly.

pressure hull
The pressure-resistant hull of a submersible.

pressurized
At an atmospheric pressure that is higher than that of the surroundings.

reconnaissance
An inspection of an area, particularly to gather military information.

renewable energy
A naturally occurring form of energy, such as wind, solar or wave power, that is in theory inexhaustible.

rig
A lorry or truck.

rollcage
A metal cage fitted around the seat of a racing car to prevent the driver being crushed if the car rolls over.

rudder
A movable blade at the stern of a boat or aircraft that can be turned to change direction.

satellite
An object that orbits a larger object. Artificial satellites orbit the Earth and provide telecommunication links and information about the Earth's surface. Natural satellites include the Moon, which orbits the Earth.

sinkhole
A depression in the surface of land, usually in limestone areas, formed by the collapse of the roof of a cavern.

sound barrier
The sudden increase in air resistance that happens to an aircraft as it approaches the speed of sound.

speedway
A road or track where high-speed driving is allowed.

stratosphere
The part of the atmosphere from 15 to 50km above the Earth's surface.

submersible
Any vessel capable of operating or remaining underwater.

supersonic
Faster than the speed of sound.

time trial
A race in which the competitors are timed individually on a set distance over the course.

titanium
A strong, corrosion-resistant metallic element used as an alloy for aircraft.

trimaran
A fast boat with three parallel hulls.

turbine
An engine in which a moving fluid, such as steam, water, hot gases or air, is converted to mechanical power.

turbojet
A jet engine that is driven by a turbine.

white-out
A complete loss of visibility because of snow or fog.

Michael Schumacher's Ferrari F248 F1 car

Index

Acknowledgements

The publisher would like to thank the following for permission to reproduce their material. Every care has been taken to trace copyright holders. However, if there have been unintentional omissions or failure to trace copyright holders, we apologize and will, if informed, endeavour to make corrections in any future edition.

Key: *b* = bottom, *c* = centre, *l* = left, *r* = right, *t* = top

Cover *front cover* Getty/AFP; Page 1 Photolibrary Erik Aeder; 2–3 iStockphoto; 4–5 Corbis/James Reeve; 7 PA/EMP; 8*tl* Getty/Hulton; 9*br* Barber Nichols Inc.; 10*l* Getty/Hulton; 10*b* Corbis/Bettman; 11*tr* NASA; 11*b* USAF; 12*tl* LAT Photographic; 12–13 Corbis/Schlegelmilch; 13*tr* Corbis/David Madison; 14*l* Corbis; 14–15 Sutton Motorsports Images; 15*tr* Getty/AFP; 16*tl* Herrenknecht AG, Germany; 16–17 Science Photo Library/Tony Craddock; 17*tr* Caterpillar Inc; 18 Shutterstock; 19*t* Getty/AFP/STR; 19*b* Alamy/ David Noble; 20*tl* PA Photos; 20–21 National Geographic Images; 22 NASA; 23*t* PA/AP; 23*b* Corbis/ Karen Kasmauski; 24–25 Shutterstock; 24*cl* SNCF Alstom Transport, France; 25*tl* Alamy/Peter Widmann; 26–27 Rex Features/Sipa Press; 27*tr* Shutterstock; 27*bl* PA/AP; 28*tl* Chris Carr; 28*lc* Fred Rompelberg, 28–29 Corbis/Tim de Waele; 29*b* Emilio Scotto; 30 Getty/Hulton; 31 PA/AP; 32*tl* Getty/Hulton; 32–33 PA/AP; 33*tl* Ken Warby; 33*tr* Philip Plisson, France; 34–35 Getty/Stone; 34*bl* Diogo Guerreiro and Flavio Jardim (Expedition DestinoAzul); 35*tr* Ian Edmondson/Barefoot Media; 36*cl* PA/AP; 36–37 Getty/ AFP/Torsten Blackwood; 37*tr* Millennium Super Yachts; 38–39 Royal Caribbean International; 40*tl* Ben & Elinore Carlin; 40–41 Rinspeed Inc., Switzerland; 41*t* Sealegs Corp. NZ; 41*b* Corbis/epa; 42 Alcoa Inc.; 43 Carnegie Mellon University; 44 Getty/Hulton; 45 NASA/Dryden; 46–47 Corbis/Philip Wallick; 48*cl* Getty/AFP; 49*tr* Corbis/How Hwee Young; 49*br* Getty/AFP; 50*tl* Bob Holloway; 50–51 Corbis/ Firefly productions; 51*br* Juergen Lehle; 52*tl* PA/AP; 52–53 PA/AP; 54*bl* PA/AP; 54–55 PA/AP; 55*tr* PA/AP; 55*br* Joseph Kittinger; 56*tl* ESA/NASA; 56*cr* Corbis/Roger Ressmeyer; 56*bl* NASA; 57 NASA; 58 PA/AP; 59 Shutterstock; 60*bl* Getty/Fred Tanneau/AFP; 60*tr* PA/AP; 61 Corbis/ Schlegelmilch; 62–63 iStockphoto; 64 Getty/Daniel Forster/AFP

The publisher would like to thank the following illustrators:
Steven Weston (Linden Artists) 8–9; Encompass Graphics 21, 34;
Peter Winfield 25, 52; Sebastian Quigley (Linden Artists) 42–43, 48–49